Deep-sea
CREEPS

A field guide to
terrible ex-boyfriends
(as sea creatures)

DANIELLE KRAESE

Smith
Street
Books

Introduction

Terrible ex-boyfriends: they're one of life's great wonders.
Or rather, it's a wonder why you dated them for as long
as you did.

Able to thrive under harsh conditions, they can be found
in the darkest depths of the ocean, the crustiest corners
of your local dive bar, and the most secluded nooks of
your DMs. If there's one thing they all have in common,
it's that you're most likely to encounter them when
you've reached rock bottom.

This field guide takes you through a wide assortment of
ex-boyfriends, reimagined as deep-sea creatures—from
The Self-Proclaimed "Nice Guy" to The Egomaniac, and
even The Ex Who Wanted To Break Up (But Wanted You
To Do It). You may already be familiar with some of these
exes—or you may have blocked them from your memory
and your social media accounts.

Researchers claim we still know very little about them,
though some might argue we've seen all we need to
see. Either way, you can sit back and enjoy these exes
from a comfortable distance. Just don't forget to
come up for air.

Nicolas

aka The Ex Who Was Too Cool For Everything

NOTABLE BEHAVIORS
Looking down his nose at anything you like

DESCRIPTION
Nicolas prides himself on his refined tastes and
is deterred by anything he considers to be too
mainstream. While he occasionally tolerated your
Love Island marathons, he was sure to let you know he
thought the show was artless and undignified. (Clearly
he wasn't really watching it.) Some researchers speculate
that Nicolas was considered profoundly uncool in high
school and has developed this behavior as a defense
mechanism. Others believe that he's just a bit of a jerk.
Either way, it took a breakthrough with your therapist
for you to finally end it with him, which you did in
person, in a mall food court. Obviously he thought that
was pretty uncool of you, on multiple levels.

RANGE
Nicolas can be found attending shows by bands you've
never heard of, eating cuisine you wouldn't appreciate,
or watching films you probably wouldn't understand.

FIG 1: *Nicolas*

FIG 2: *Gio*

Gio

aka The Ex With A Heart Of Ice

NOTABLE BEHAVIORS
Scowling; grunting; frowning

DESCRIPTION
Unable to tolerate anything earnest or heartfelt,
Gio is grouchy beyond his years. He prefers to live
on cynicism and is repelled by the sound of a child's
joyful laughter. For some reason, he especially hated
the sound of you giggling at TikToks while lying in bed
next to him. (You thought he was already awake!) You
knew it was over when you showed him a video of a
Shiba Inu who is best friends with a tortoise, and all he
had to say in response was, "For crying out loud, will
you just let me sleep?"

NESTING
Gio is always yelling at kids to get off his lawn,
even though he doesn't actually have one.

Simon

aka The Ex Who Disappeared When
It Was Time To Meet Your Family

NOTABLE BEHAVIORS
Hunting for excuses; darting out of sight

DESCRIPTION
As far as boyfriends go, Simon is the kind of guy who
will always be there for you—until it's time to meet
your family. Then he's nowhere to be found. Simon
has the ability to sense when relatives are approaching
and make a quick escape, usually with some kind of
nonsensical excuse, like he forgot to turn off his iron.
(This might be more believable if the man's clothes
didn't always look like crepe paper.) You and Simon
once bumped into your sister at IKEA, and he changed
colors before scrambling inside a KLEPPSTAD
sliding wardrobe with adjustable shelving. He may
still be in there.

RANGE
Simon has lied about being in dozens of different
countries to avoid meeting someone's parents.

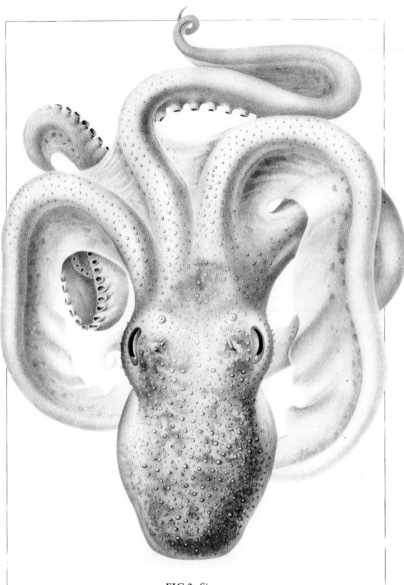

FIG 3: *Simon*

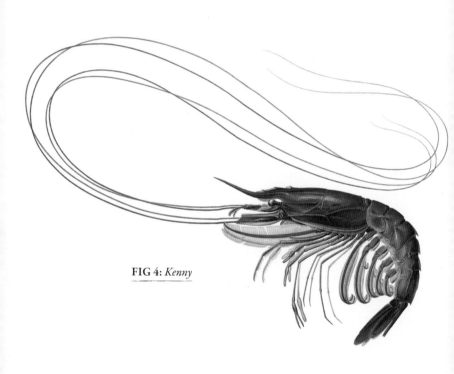

FIG 4: *Kenny*

Kenny

aka The Self-Proclaimed "Nice Guy"

NOTABLE BEHAVIORS
*Boasting about things that decent people just do
(e.g., listening when women speak, supporting gender
equality, being kind to the elderly)*

DESCRIPTION
Kenny is always being overlooked—at least that's
what Kenny says. Known for his ability to camouflage,
he attracts mates by disguising himself as a nice guy.
You first bonded with him over your mutual love of
video games, and he was impressed by your knack for
urban planning when playing *Animal Crossing*. But
you told him you weren't ready to get serious because
you were still getting over a breakup (Amber and Greg
from Season 5 of *Love Island UK*). Kenny responded
by telling you that you're not that hot anyway, and
that your *Animal Crossing* islanders all seemed
bored and unfulfilled.

RANGE
Kenny claims he is always relegated to "The Friend
Zone", a region that, researchers have proven,
doesn't actually exist.

Karl

aka The Ex Who Never Deactivated His Tinder Profile

NOTABLE BEHAVIORS
Keeping his eyes out for something better

DESCRIPTION
Karl will not hesitate to define the relationship.
He's just reluctant to let go of his dating apps. When
you first noticed his Tinder was still active, a week
into your relationship, it seemed harmless enough.
(You only saw it because you were logging on to
deactivate yours—he was probably about to do the
same!) But upon further observation, you realized
he was still gathering new thirst traps and portraits
of himself holding large fish. As for his bio, he
continued to update it by adding more and more
quotes from *Pulp Fiction*. That's when you knew your
relationship couldn't go on any longer. (Eventually,
he was going to make you watch *Pulp Fiction*.)

FEEDING HABITS
Researchers estimate that Karl's fridge must contain
at least 80 pounds of largemouth bass.

FIG 5: *Karl*

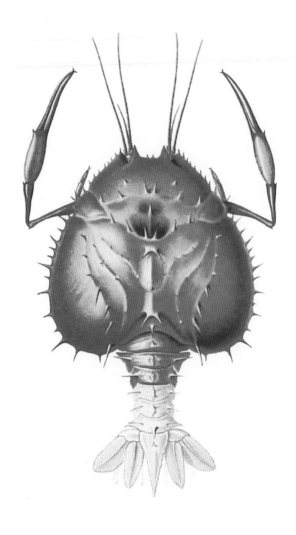

FIG 6: *Randall*

Randall

aka The Ex Who Nickel-And-Dimed You

NOTABLE BEHAVIORS
Maintaining a running tab of things you owe him for

DESCRIPTION

From birth, Randall has had the largest bank account of any creature in this guide. (His parents are wealthy condiment heirs who never deny him anything.) Yet he always appears to be pinching pennies. The first time you stayed over at his apartment, he asked if you would start chipping in for utilities. And during a trip to the beach, you watched him wrestle a kid over a coin in the sand that turned out to be a bottlecap. Still, he had his tender moments. He let you cry on his shoulder when you lost your job—he even gave you a clean tissue from his pocket. Of course, the next day, he sent you a $1 invoice for "hanky reimbursement".

NESTING

Randall recently finished renovations on his bathroom. It's now a pay toilet.

Mario

aka The Ex Who Wanted To Break Up
(But Wanted You To Do It)

NOTABLE BEHAVIORS
Picking fights; flaking on plans; hiding

DESCRIPTION
Still a juvenile specimen, Mario has a hard time
opening up in relationships. Especially when he wants
them to end. Instead of initiating a breakup himself, he
prefers strategic relationship sabotage—this technique
makes dating him so annoying that his partner is forced
to dump him. What Mario didn't anticipate was that
you were used to dating insufferable men, so it took
six months for you to notice all his efforts. What
finally did it was him deliberately spoiling the ending
of *Breaking Bad* for you. (You hadn't actually started
watching it, but he knew you were planning to get
to it, someday.)

RANGE
Mario will go to the ends of the earth to avoid
having an uncomfortable conversation.

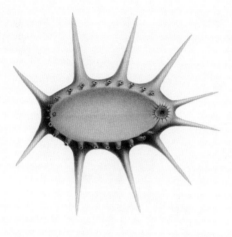

FIG 6: *Mario*

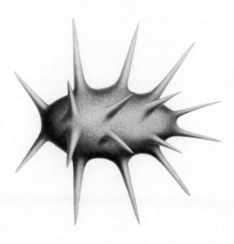

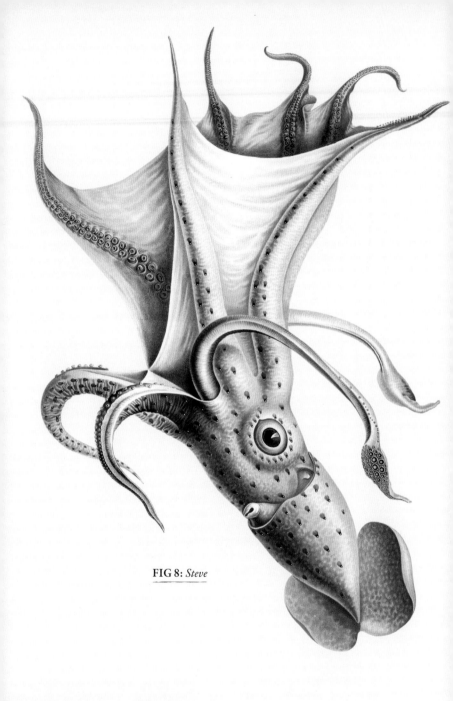

FIG 8: *Steve*

Steve

aka The Ex With A Wandering Eye

NOTABLE BEHAVIORS
Winking; whistling; giving elevator eyes

DESCRIPTION
For better or worse, Steve is considered the "friendliest" creature in the ocean. As your boyfriend, he was known for his elaborate displays of courtship with people who were not you. Everyone appears to be his type. To his credit, he was always honest with you about which of your friends he thought were hot, and which of your friends he thought were *really* hot. If only he paid you that level of attention, maybe he would have noticed when you made the conscious transition from high-rise jeans to mid-rise jeans. (You really could have used some emotional support during that fraught time.)

MATING RITUALS
Steve's not ruling anyone out just yet.

Josef

aka The Ex Who Pretended To Be Totally Helpless

NOTABLE BEHAVIORS
Shrugging cluelessly; waiting for someone else to do it

DESCRIPTION
Many of the creatures in this guide dabble in weaponized incompetence, but for Josef, it's his primary defense mechanism. Case in point: Despite being a respected electrical engineer, he claims he doesn't know how to run his own dishwasher. Dating Josef meant living with an endless list of unanswerable questions, like: Where is your toilet paper? Have you washed these sheets since ever? Why do all of the dishes smell like hand sanitizer? When you broke it off with Josef, he pretended not to understand—so technically, you may actually still be together.

FEEDING HABITS
Josef has remarkable culinary skills, which he conceals by starting small, deliberate kitchen fires.

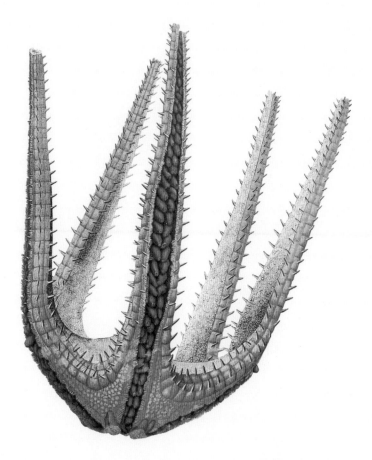

FIG 9: *Josef*

FIG 10: *Rob*

Rob

aka The Mansplainer

NOTABLE BEHAVIORS
*Clearing his throat, like he's ready to interrupt
at any moment; beginning every utterance with,
"Well, actually..."*

DESCRIPTION
Positioning himself as the expert on everything, Rob
is quick to condescend upon his prey. He may display
an infuriating sense of overconfidence, but this behavior
is designed to protect his fragile ego. Rob once loudly
argued that you were wrong about the spelling of your
own family name—at least he could have waited to
raise this concern until after your brother's wedding
ceremony. But to be fair, you probably should have
waited until after the reception to dump him. (You told
him it was the final straw, though he still insists it was
the third or fourth straw, at most.)

RANGE
Despite there being a lack of evidence,
Rob believes he's above everyone else.

Curtis

aka The Party Boy

NOTABLE BEHAVIORS
*Hopping from bar to bar; pumping his fist to
the beat; chugging Vodka Red Bulls*

DESCRIPTION
Most active at night, Curtis conserves energy
during the day by sleeping through all of it. Then he
awakens ready to rave. While other creatures in this
guide exhibit similar behaviors before fully maturing,
Curtis may never grow out of it. Some observers note
he can be incredibly rowdy after sucking up too many
Kamikaze shots—but that's actually just his personality.
Things got weird between you when, during a wild
night out with "the boys", he texted a butt pic to your
mom (and not even a particularly good one). These
days, the only contact you have is his regular "u up?"
messages, which usually come at 7 a.m., as you're
polishing off your overnight oats.

RANGE
Curtis is currently banned from six clubs, two dive bars,
and all McDonald's locations.

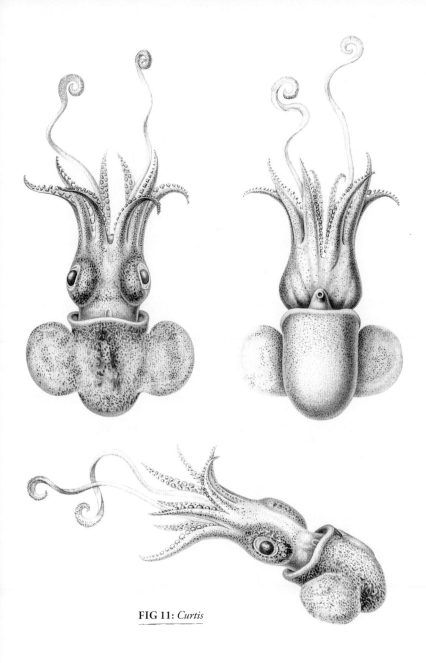

FIG 11: *Curtis*

FIG 12: *Theo*

Theo

aka The Improv Star

NOTABLE BEHAVIORS
*Being drawn to any strong source of light
(e.g., the spotlight, the limelight, the ring light)*

DESCRIPTION
Theo treats every waking moment as part of a "bit".
This is because being a performer is in his DNA
(his parents were in a vacuum commercial in the '90s).
At first, you found his constant playfulness refreshing.
But you soon realized it was impossible to discuss
anything serious with him, like where things were
going, whether you were exclusive, or why he hadn't
liked the latest Instagram post from your Jamie Foxx
appreciation account. Over time, it became clear
that being part of his permanent ensemble would
"zip zap zop" the life out of you.

APPEARANCE
Theo is often seen with experimental facial hair and
long-sleeve flannel shirts, regardless of climate.

Arman

aka The Egomaniac

NOTABLE BEHAVIORS
*Smoldering; posing; letting every compliment
go straight to his head*

DESCRIPTION
Easily recognized by his enormous ego, Arman
thinks everyone he encounters wants to get with him.
The most annoying part is, he's usually right.
He tends to draw attention wherever he goes because
he's downright mesmerizing. Arman feeds on
compliments, and ultimately, you had a hard time
keeping up with his ego's appetite. Also, would it have
killed him to send a compliment your way here and
there? It was like he didn't even notice that time you got
buzzed off one-and-a-half hard seltzers and decided to
give yourself curtain bangs. Arman described breaking
up with you as a "humanitarian act". (He felt other
people deserved a chance to date him, too.)

NESTING
When it comes to his taste in decor, Arman is drawn
to anything with a reflective surface.

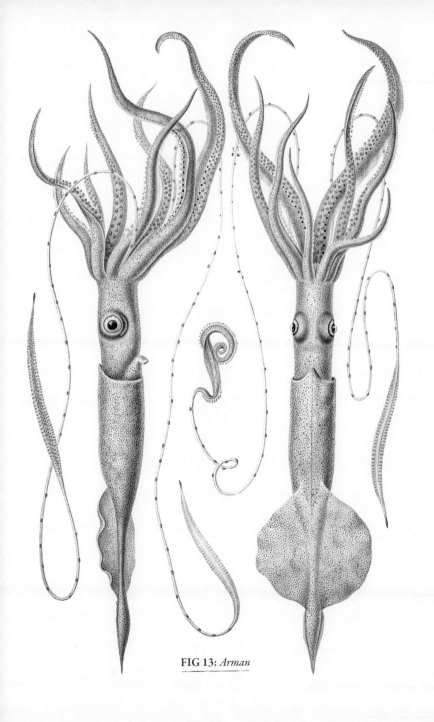

FIG 13: *Arman*

FIG 14: *Francisco*

Francisco

aka The Ex Who Took Himself Way Too Seriously

NOTABLE BEHAVIORS
*Sighing; glaring in disapproval; shaking his head
at your childishness*

DESCRIPTION
Francisco is as serious as the list of side effects rattled
off at the end of a prescription medication commercial.
He thinks kittens are frivolous, and he didn't like
Dunkirk because he found it too lighthearted. Your
friends said you were a strange pairing from the start—
after all, he's a no-nonsense tax auditor, and you're
someone who once enrolled in a class called "Clown
Work For Improvisers". Francisco could not tolerate
any of your cheesy puns, and it wasn't long before
you started to get feta up. (He didn't laugh at that
one either.) Also, your dog never warmed to him, and
Bone Iver is usually a good judge of character.

APPEARANCE
Francisco spends every waking hour in a suit.
He doesn't have any sleeping hours. (He says dreaming
is for the overindulgent.)

Landon (and Brandon)

aka The Package Deal

NOTABLE BEHAVIORS

Procuring movie tickets in threes; saying "I'll check if Brandon's free" any time you ask him to hang out

DESCRIPTION

Whenever you spot Landon in the wild, you can be certain that Brandon isn't far off. These two creatures are deeply bonded and also former frat brothers. They can be most easily identified by their matching bicep tattoos that say "best friends" in a language neither of them can read or speak. At first, you were charmed by their symbiotic relationship. But eventually, you got tired of Brandon tagging along on all of your dates—and interrupting you and Landon during sex to ask if you wanted to watch *American Idol* (even if you did). In the end, someone had to be voted out of this threesome. (Spoiler: It was you.)

FEEDING HABITS

Landon and Brandon have not eaten a meal apart since their college dining hall days. And their diets have not evolved since then either (it's mostly room temperature chicken nuggets).

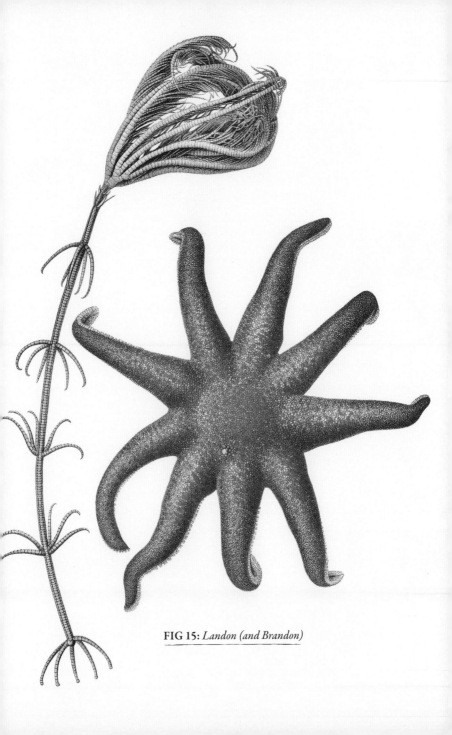

FIG 15: *Landon (and Brandon)*

FIG 16: *Tyler*

Tyler

aka The Projector

NOTABLE BEHAVIORS
Misdirection; pointing a finger at you

DESCRIPTION
Highly toxic. Tyler is one of the fastest creatures to direct blame at someone else, whether it's for passing gas, leaving the freezer door open, or forgetting his mom's birthday. He always suspected you were cheating on him, but this was only because he was cheating on you (with just about everyone he knew). Unfortunately for Tyler, deception isn't one of his natural abilities. He was quickly exposed when he used your laptop to google "cheating without getting caught how to do". Of course, he responded by accusing you of always forgetting to clear your browser history.

RANGE
Researchers are still studying Tyler to better understand just how low he can stoop.

Roger

aka The Ex Who Was Obsessed With Getting Free Stuff

NOTABLE BEHAVIORS
Sneaking into events just for the gift bags; picking at the remains of lost and founds

DESCRIPTION
Roger has a cushy lifestyle, yet his main source of energy comes from getting things for free. He can often be seen wearing promotional merch for companies he's never heard of, and he has the largest collection of reusable tote bags of any creature in this guide. (He got them complimentary after purchasing items that he immediately returned.) Whenever you went out to eat together, he would make a small scene while stealing all the condiments off the table … despite being allergic to mustard. One time, a packet of ketchup exploded in his pocket—fortunately, he was wearing a shirt he "found" in your closet.

FEEDING HABITS
Roger will eat almost anything, as long as you're paying.

FIG 17: *Roger*

FIG 18: *Naveen*

Naveen

aka The Ex Who Was Threatened By Your Success

NOTABLE BEHAVIORS
Competing for resources; stealing thunder

DESCRIPTION
While he has his charms, Naveen is easily provoked by other people's achievements. When he feels threatened, he reacts with elaborate displays of one-upmanship that can stun his prey into an awkward silence. Naveen became prickly when anything good happened for you—even just finding a ripe avocado at the market. When you took a novel-writing workshop, suddenly he was working on a novel, too. And he is still miffed about the time you got an email from a Nigerian prince looking to share his fortune with you (even though His Royal Highness stopped responding when you asked if he could instead use his influence to get your dog more followers on Instagram). Dating a man who couldn't handle your success forced you to ask yourself some really tough questions. Like, "Since when am I successful?"

RANGE
There's no limit to how far Naveen will go to outdo someone.

Neil

aka The Man Child

NOTABLE BEHAVIORS
Playing games; refusing to share; throwing food

DESCRIPTION
Though fully grown and capable, Neil has proven
reluctant to embrace certain adult habits, like paying his
bills, cleaning his toilet, and cutting his toenails. He has
the ability to wash dishes and put them away—he just
prefers to leave them in the sink to collect sediment.
Neil typically seeks out parasitic relationships with
mates who can tolerate doing everything for him.
And he isn't quite ready for a mature relationship.
When you were together, he was easily frightened
by his own feelings. He once told you he was falling
in love with you—then, after a nervous second, he
yelled "PSYCH!" and gave you a wedgie.

NESTING
Neil has not lived with his mom for years, but he
still "visits" regularly with a load of dirty laundry
for her to wash.

FIG 19: *Neil*

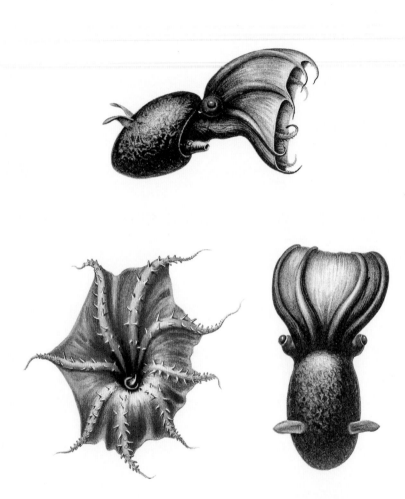

FIG 20: *Wyatt*

Wyatt

aka The Travel Snob

NOTABLE BEHAVIORS
*Slipping foreign phrases into casual conversation;
displaying hashtags like #wanderlust and
#DoYouEvenTravelBro*

DESCRIPTION
Wyatt can be difficult to find, as he's always on the
move. Known for his showy migratory patterns, he has
been all over the globe and looks down on anyone who
hasn't. (Never mind that some people don't have the
same access to his dad's American Express Platinum
Card.) Wyatt is quick to tell anyone who didn't ask that
he's inking the next *On the Road.* While you couldn't
afford to keep up with his travels, you had already
seen much of the world through illegally streaming
every *Love Island* franchise. Despite your worldliness,
Wyatt eventually broke up with you. He said he
wanted to be monogamous with the planet.

RANGE
Pretty much everywhere. The only place left on Wyatt's
bucket list is a remote corner of Antarctica.

Cameron

aka The Ex Who Wasn't The Guy You Thought He Was

NOTABLE BEHAVIORS
*Dodging personal questions; posting abstract photos
on Instagram with cryptic captions*

DESCRIPTION
Cameron is notoriously difficult to identify.
It's not even clear how old he is—he could be 25, he
could be 45. Your friends and family didn't know
what to make of him. You often found yourself saying,
"You just have to get to know him!" But Cameron is
unknowable by design. Researchers believe he's wanted
in multiple territories for posing online as a middle-
aged mom with a phony multi-level marketing company
(somehow taking an already fraudulent hustle and
finding a way to make it even more deceptive). What
disappointed you most was not that he disappeared
without a goodbye, but that you never received your
bulk order of that Moroccan Superfood Hand Cream
he told you about—it really did sound life-changing.

HABITAT
Cameron does not live in a permanent pad, but instead
hops from one extravagant Airbnb to another.

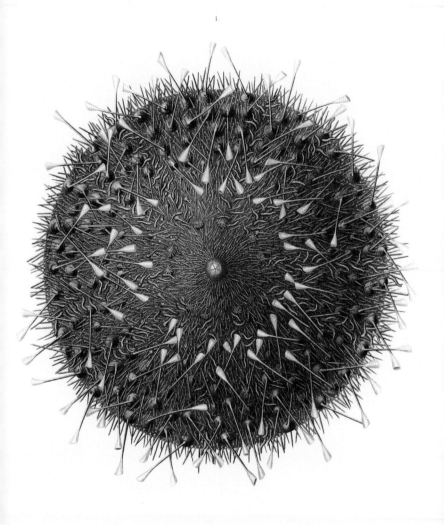

FIG 21: *Cameron*

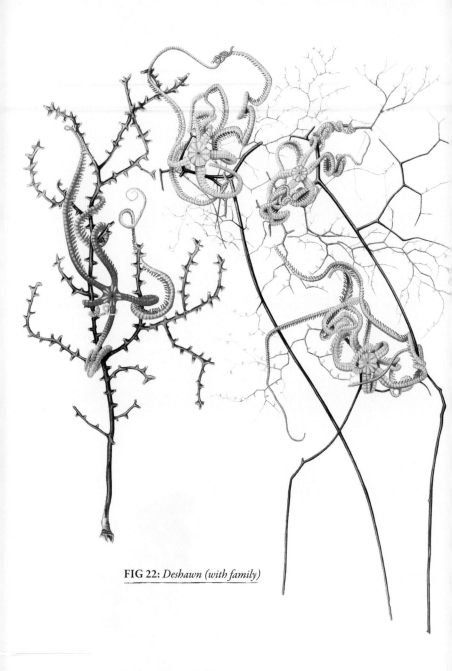

FIG 22: *Deshawn (with family)*

Deshawn

aka The Ex Who Was A Little Too Close To His Family

NOTABLE BEHAVIORS
Leaving the door open for drop-ins; engaging in Full House-style group hugs

DESCRIPTION
Upon reaching maturity, Deshawn moved out of his childhood home to live on his own. But now he is more entangled with his family than ever. His dad is his boss, his mom is his landlord, and his brother is always sleeping over on the couch (even though he lives in the equally nice apartment next door). When they're not all together, they communicate constantly through an elaborate series of memes exchanged in the group chat. Whenever you had an argument, he'd invite his family to come over and weigh in. You wouldn't have minded if they had taken your side every now and then.

RANGE
It has been confirmed that Deshawn and his family have no boundaries whatsoever.

Jackson

aka The Ex Who Never Stopped Networking

NOTABLE BEHAVIORS
*Climbing the career ladder; sharing his Google Calendar
so you can put some time on it*

DESCRIPTION
Jackson sees every encounter as a networking
opportunity, even though it's still not known what he
does for work or even what his skills are. He loves to
work a room and is always reaching out to offer a firm
handshake with eye contact. Jackson passes out business
cards faster than you can say, "Please stop, this is my
grandfather's funeral." Immediately after meeting your
parents, he sent them a request to connect on LinkedIn.
(You didn't even know they had accounts.) While your
relationship didn't last, he still reaches out periodically
to ask if he can use you as a reference.

MATING RITUALS
Jackson doesn't want kids, but someday he would love
to have a startup that's really more like a family.

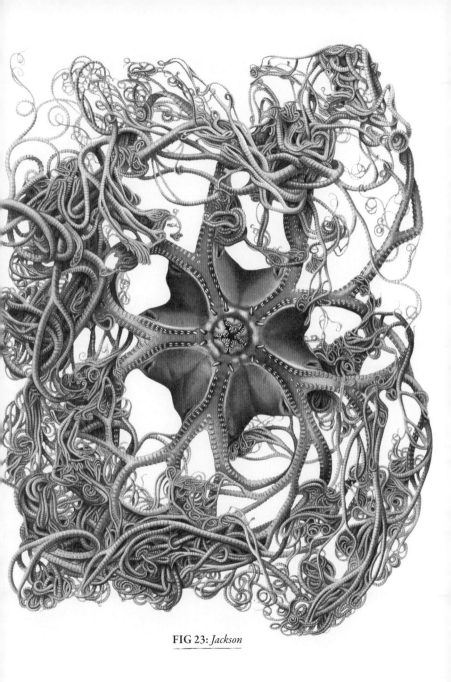

FIG 23: *Jackson*

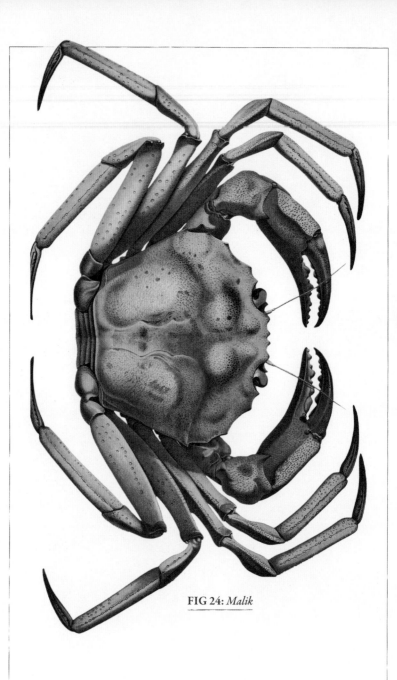

FIG 24: *Malik*

Malik

aka The Ex Who Made A Big Deal About Your
"Age Gap"

NOTABLE BEHAVIORS
*Grasping at straws; describing things as being
"before your time"*

DESCRIPTION
Malik was really fixated on the fact that you were
younger than him—10 months younger, to be exact.
Whenever he did something that didn't make sense to
you, like wearing socks with sandals, leaving dishes to
"soak" overnight, or refusing to watch *The Great British
Bake Off*, he'd say defensively, "When you're my age,
you'll understand." When you were the first one to start
getting lower back pain, Malik became weirdly jealous.
You dated him for 10 months—just long enough to
confirm that you still didn't understand him (except
for the socks with sandals thing... that's actually pretty
comfy). Since then, you stopped seeing Malik and
started seeing an orthopedist.

NESTING
As far as researchers can tell, those dishes
are still soaking.

Anthony

aka The Ex Who Didn't Want Feminism
To Go "Too Far"

NOTABLE BEHAVIORS
Marching for men's rights

DESCRIPTION
Anthony thinks equality is great—just as long as
women don't become *too* equal. He will be the first
to say he doesn't have a misogynistic bone in his
body. Don't believe him? Just ask his "female doctor".
(Yes, he always calls her that.) He's never read a book
that wasn't written by a man ... but he likes that they
exist. Biologists suspect that Anthony may never
develop self-awareness. To his credit, when you were
together, he never minimized your emotions, unless
he felt you were being overemotional.

MATING RITUALS
Anthony supports "girl bosses", but prefers a partner
who will also be his girl maid.

FIG 25: *Anthony*

FIG 26: *Luke*

Luke

aka The Ex Who Was A Nightmare At Restaurants

NOTABLE BEHAVIORS
Leaving a trail of one-star Yelp reviews

DESCRIPTION
Luke calls himself a foodie, but at the restaurants he patronizes, he's better known as the Devil In Zip-Off Cargo Shorts. Frequently found talking down to waitstaff, he does not hesitate to send a dish back if it isn't prepared exactly to his liking (instead of devouring the entire thing out of guilt and pretending it's what he wanted all along, like a normal person). All this pretension, coming from a man you watched burn microwave popcorn every single time he made it. The last time you ever went over to his place, you told him you found him wholly unsavory and would not be coming back, ever.

RANGE
Luke goes everywhere by way of his high horse.

Keegan

aka The Ex Who Loved To Dish It But Couldn't Take It

NOTABLE BEHAVIORS
Administering burns, negs, and disses

DESCRIPTION

Keegan's courtship displays have not evolved much since he was in elementary school. He is unable to produce a genuine compliment—instead, he expresses his love through relentless put-downs disguised as affectionate jokes. Sometimes, he didn't even realize he was doing it, like when you suggested he see a doctor for his visible toe infection and he said, "Wow, that's actually a smart idea." Despite all his zingers, Keegan has very thin skin and couldn't handle you giving it back to him. When you saw him drive for the first time, you told him he did pretty good for a man, and he never spoke to you again.

FEEDING HABITS

The only thing Keegan can't tolerate is a taste of his own medicine.

FIG 27: *Keegan*

FIG 28: *Vlad*

Vlad

aka The Ex Who Was Always Disappearing

NOTABLE BEHAVIORS
Going into hiding; leaving his partners on read

DESCRIPTION

Vlad keeps his relationships exciting by going totally off-grid without warning. Sometimes he'd respond to your texts right away. Other times he wouldn't answer for so long you'd become certain he must have died in a tragic accident. You would be in the middle of drafting a really moving eulogy when he'd resurface, eight days later, with a casual "wyd". What was he doing during those times he went missing? Did he have a whole other "babe", with whom he shared a whole other backlog of legal dramas to watch on Netflix? Also, and this was a separate issue, why hadn't you ever actually seen him brush his teeth? Researchers still don't have the answers (except for that last one— he definitely isn't brushing).

MATING RITUALS
Vlad reels in potential mates by keeping them on unsteady footing.

Leo

aka The Ex Who Was A Bit Too Laidback

NOTABLE BEHAVIORS
*Taking his time; going with the flow;
playing everything by ear*

DESCRIPTION
Spontaneous and unpredictable, Leo is incapable
of committing to plans. He prefers to just see where
the day takes him. His personal mantra is "No
worries, my dude!", though his actions (or inactions)
cause an abundance of worries for all the "dudes"
around him. Sometimes he just didn't show up
to things, like your *Dancing with the Stars* watch
party. And sometimes he crashed things he wasn't
invited to, like your sister's home birth (for some
reason, he brought a 12-pack of Corona). When
his toilet flooded his apartment, instead of calling
his super to fix it, he just started wearing rain boots
inside. That's around the time you realized your
relationship was taking on too much water.

HABITAT
Leo lives in total darkness because he never bothered
to buy a lamp for his apartment.

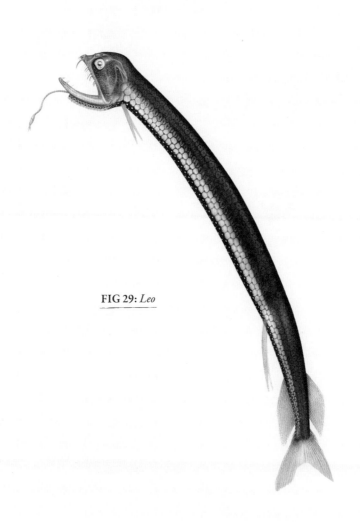

FIG 29: *Leo*

FIG 30: *Charles*

Charles

aka The Ex Who Loves Making Big Future Plans
(But Won't Commit To Plans This Weekend)

NOTABLE BEHAVIORS
Being all over the place

DESCRIPTION
Charles attracts his mates by romanticizing about the
future, but he has no plans to follow through in the
present. He was always brainstorming names for your
hypothetical children. He even planned to handle the
childcare so you could pursue your dream of opening
a little boutique that sells daytime pajamas. (Everyone
would call them "timeless".) But if you asked him to
commit to plans that week, he'd get dodgy. You finally
had it the night he blew off your karaoke birthday
party. You ended up getting drunk and leaving him
a voicemail that was just you sob-singing Lizzo's
"Truth Hurts". It's fair to say that ended things on
a bad note.

FEEDING HABITS
Charles will sooner plan his future wedding menu
than agree to dinner plans next week.

Garrett

aka The Ex With Two Faces

NOTABLE BEHAVIORS
Dragging his partners behind their backs

DESCRIPTION
From a distance, Garrett has the appearance of the
ideal boyfriend—or at least a fairly harmless one. But
closer observation will reveal he's the type to gripe to
his buds about the "ol' ball and chain". In his group
chat, he loved making fun of you for reminding him to
do his taxes. And you once overheard him describe you
as a nag for suggesting he needed a stronger password
for his online banking accounts. (For the record, the
password was "GARRETT".) Your breakup with
Garrett was mutual and cordial—he wished you all
the best and even let you keep his NutriBullet blender.
Then he told his friends he dumped you for being a
"crazy kitchen appliance thief".

MATING RITUALS
Garrett is only interested in tying the knot so he can
have an excuse to make "take my wife, please" jokes.

FIG 31: *Garrett*

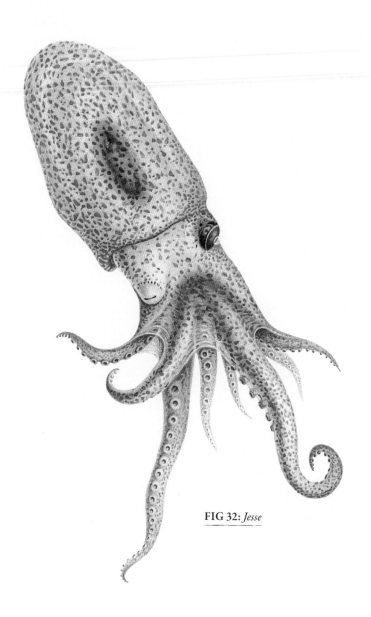

FIG 32: *Jesse*

Jesse

aka The Ex Who Won't Let Go Of His
High School Days

NOTABLE BEHAVIORS
Hanging on to the past; wearing his high school colors

DESCRIPTION
Jesse is always grasping at the glory of his youth.
He has been known to yell out "Go Bulldogs!" totally
unprovoked, and he will seek out any opportunity to
mention he had the time of his life at winter formal.
(We get it—he was cool in high school.) When you
were seeing Jesse, his idea of the perfect date was
driving around together all night with six of his friends
piled into the back of his sedan. Sometimes he'd
get a mischievous look and ask if you wanted to go
smoke cigarettes together in the woods. You didn't,
but as someone who was spectacularly uncool in high
school, it was nice to finally be invited.

HABITAT
A shrine to his 17-year-old self, Jesse's bedroom
still contains a bewildering assortment of varsity
bowling trophies.

Kai

aka The Ex Who Still Wasn't Over His Ex

NOTABLE BEHAVIORS
Living in denial; not-so-quietly yearning

DESCRIPTION

Even a casual observer can see that Kai has not moved past his last relationship. For starters, he still likes all of his ex's Instagram posts. And before bed, he can be observed scrolling through his phone, looking at the criminally unflattering candids he took of her when they were together. Whenever you suggested Kai might still have feelings for his ex, he would become highly defensive. Sometimes he'd even accuse you of being insecure and jealous, which was uncalled for and entirely accurate. You finally had enough when he called you his ex's name in a moment of heated passion. (You had just blown him up with a red shell while playing *Mario Kart*.)

NESTING

Kai still displays framed photos of his ex around his apartment. (Until recently, researchers did not think 20-something men even had printed photos.)

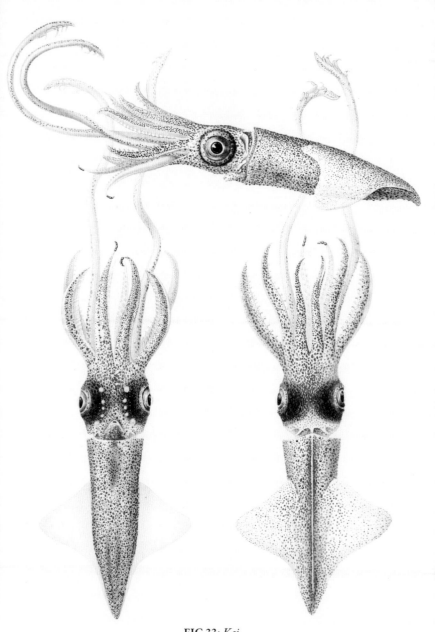

FIG 33: *Kai*

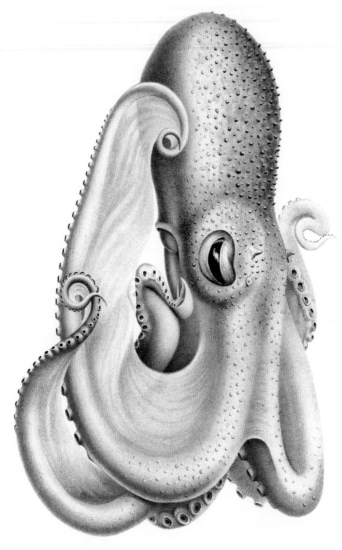

FIG 34: *Brad*

Brad

aka The Ex Who Was Enamored With
The Sound Of His Own Voice

NOTABLE BEHAVIORS
Talking over, under, and around everyone he encounters

DESCRIPTION
One of the many creatures in this guide possessing an
overgrown ego, Brad has been known to give himself
goosebumps when he speaks. He can tolerate listening
to others for as long as several seconds before cutting
them off with a totally unrelated anecdote or "factoid".
And he moves quickly if he senses an opportunity to
make a speech. After a few months together, you tried
telling Brad that you needed some space. But he just
kept interrupting you to explain the plot of the movie
The Martian (which you already knew, because you
saw it in theaters with him. Twice).

NESTING
Brad converted his studio apartment into a sound stage,
so he can record his new advice podcast, *Brad Medicine*.
Brad is the only guest—and the only listener.

Miguel

aka The Ex Who Was Too Shy To Even Look At You

NOTABLE BEHAVIORS
Sweating profusely; scampering off in fright

DESCRIPTION
Whenever you tried to approach Miguel in public, he would give you a quick, nervous smile from behind his books and dart away. To be fair, you were both in seventh grade (and you haven't spoken since you reached adulthood—maybe he doesn't do this anymore). But it was tough to build a relationship with someone who could only talk to you over AOL Instant Messenger, in the hours after lacrosse practice but before his bedtime. This relationship was doomed from the moment Miguel asked his best friend to pass your best friend a note asking if you would go out with him, yes or no. But you still have the Pokémon keychain he gave you as a symbol of his like.

RANGE
While his current whereabouts are unknown, Miguel was previously limited to regions his dad was willing to take him to in the family minivan.

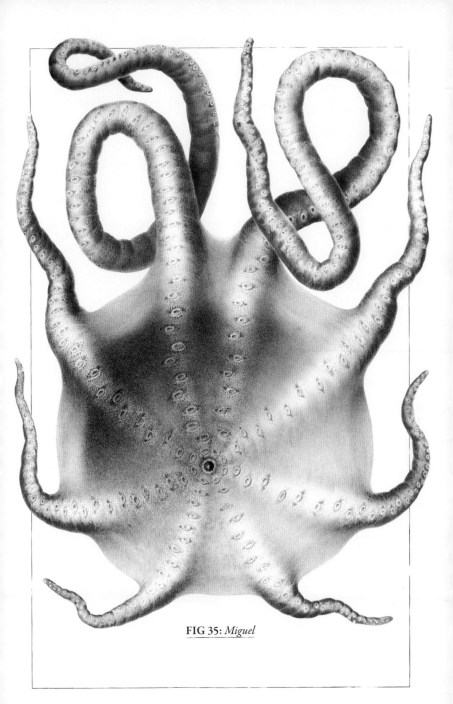

FIG 35: *Miguel*

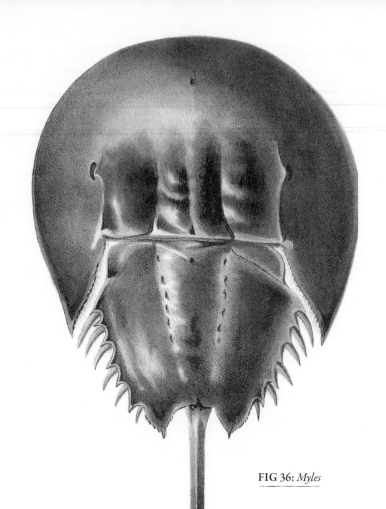

FIG 36: *Myles*

Myles

aka The Ex Who Was Stuck In His Ways

NOTABLE BEHAVIORS
Doubling down; refusing to evolve

DESCRIPTION

Myles is as rigid and uncompromising as they come. Having spent most of adulthood living in bachelor solitude, he never learned how to coexist with a mate—and it doesn't seem like he cares to. Myles wants everything to adhere to his precise specifications, from the volume of the TV to the configuration of his couch pillows. When disturbed, he will let out a soft but devastating sigh. Ultimately, it was your incompatible schedules that drove things to an end. He insisted on going to sleep at 8 p.m. sharp, so he could wake up early and go for an energizing run. You preferred to stay up all night feasting on mindless internet garbage so you could spend the next day wondering why you felt so terrible. And he just wouldn't respect that.

RANGE
Myles won't budge a millimeter.

Ray

aka The Ex Who Rushes Into Things
(And Then Rushes Right Out Of Them)

NOTABLE BEHAVIORS
Quickly catching (and releasing) feelings

DESCRIPTION
Ray has been known to dive into every romance headfirst but will flee as soon as his feelings get too serious. On your second date, he told you he loved you. And on your fourth date, he told you he had fallen out of love with you. Fortunately, you never allowed yourself to get too invested in Ray—your Pinterest wedding board was still in its early stages, and you had only taken three or four online quizzes to see what your kids would look like.

NESTING
Ray has invited dozens of love interests to move in with him, only to immediately change the locks on them.

FIG 37: *Ray*

FIG 38: *Ethan (with his "sister")*

Ethan

aka The Ex Who Failed To Mention He Was Married

NOTABLE BEHAVIORS
Burying the lede; hiding in plain sight

DESCRIPTION
To the untrained eye, Ethan appears to be a real catch. Unfortunately, he didn't tell you he'd already been caught. You were initially drawn to him because he seemed to have it all together. His clothes were stylish and tidy, his home was clean and beautifully decorated, and his fridge was always full of fresh fruit—in retrospect, it seems so obvious he had a wife. The most humiliating part was, he really had you convinced it was his sister in all those photos on his gallery wall. (You thought it was sweet that they did a professional beach photoshoot in coordinated formal wear.)

NESTING
Ethan doesn't make his own bed, but he seems to do a lot of lying in it.

Oscar

aka The Ex Who Had A Weird Thing For Your Mom

NOTABLE BEHAVIORS
*Lingering at family barbecues; calling your mom
just to say hi*

DESCRIPTION
Oscar is a creature of mature tastes—he is drawn
to things like fine wine, classic jazz, and supportive
footwear. And, while you were dating, he also appeared
to have a major thing for your retiree mother. Oscar
would become flustered whenever your mom dropped
by your place after her Sunday Zumba class. And he
started attending more of your family events than
you did. Oscar was an old-fashioned guy, so when
things became more serious, he asked your dad for his
blessing... to take your mom out. That's when you were
finally forced to end the family affair.

FEEDING HABITS
Oscar will dutifully consume any food your mom
offers to fix for him (even if he just ate).

FIG 39: *Oscar*

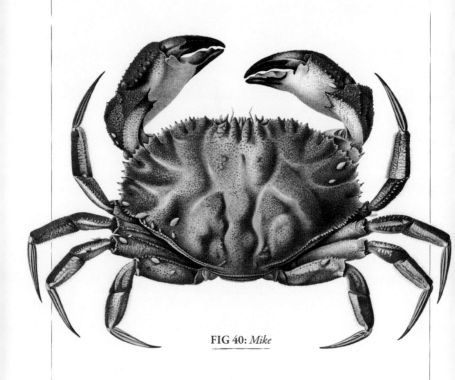

FIG 40: *Mike*

Mike

aka The Fitness Fanatic Who Wanted You
To Be One Too

NOTABLE BEHAVIORS
Waking up early; having no rest days;
drinking water on purpose

DESCRIPTION
Mike is most easily identified by his intricate displays of
getting swole. He feeds on sick gains and leaves a trail
of dirty gym towels wherever he goes. This ex-boyfriend
can often be found bragging about how much he can
lift—though, funny, when you lived together, he didn't
lift a finger outside of the gym. When you met him, you
were upfront about your fitness goals: You don't have
any. Despite this, he always begged you to try bulking
up with him. You told him you'd consider it, as soon as
he'd try bulk ordering more paper towels without you
having to remind him seven times.

MATING RITUALS
Mike is still searching for someone to share
his gym guest pass with.

Hector

aka The Ex Who Always Reeled You Back In

NOTABLE BEHAVIORS
*Keeping his hooks in you; conserving his efforts
until they're needed*

DESCRIPTION
Deliberate and cunning, Hector will avoid exerting
any more energy in a relationship than he needs to.
He could always sense when you were getting ready
to dump him, and that's when he would turn on the
charm—he'd take you out to new restaurants, shower
you with Instagram engagement, and stock his fridge
with all of your favorite non-dairy milks. (Normally,
he refused to acknowledge that some occasions call
for almond milk and some call for oat milk.) One
time, when things were really getting rocky, he asked
you to marry him. That one really bought
him some more time.

RANGE
Hector will go the distance, but he would
really prefer not to.

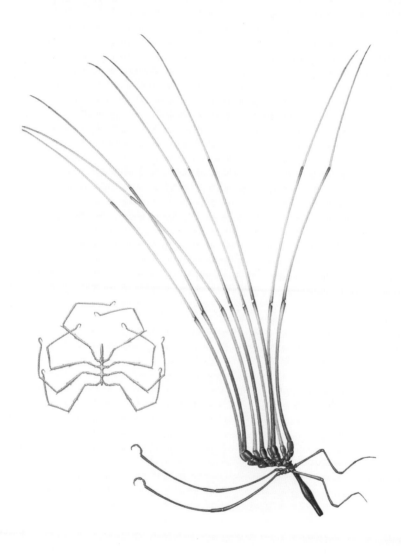

FIG 41: *Hector*

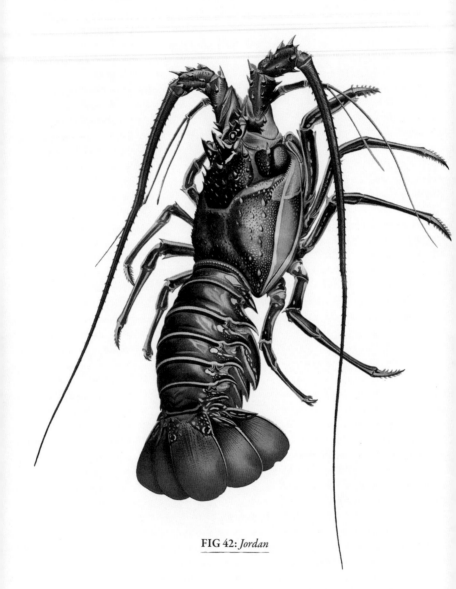

FIG 42: *Jordan*

Jordan

aka The Ex Who Was Full Of Unsolicited Opinions

NOTABLE BEHAVIORS
Chiming in when absolutely no one asked

DESCRIPTION

Busy and determined, Jordan spends most of his time spreading his unwanted opinions around. He had something to say about everything from your taste in movies to your attempts at keeping up with the latest eyebrow trends. Of course, you couldn't be offended, because he always followed it up with, "No offense." Jordan thought you looked prettier without "all that makeup on", but on the days you went barefaced, he would say you looked sick. Eventually, you decided to seize the opportunity—you told him you *were* indeed very sick and that your doctor recommended you isolate from him forever.

MATING RITUALS

Jordan would never beat around the bush—but he did once tell a partner that he preferred they keep things "a little more tidy down there".

Blake

aka The Buzzkill

NOTABLE BEHAVIORS
Raining on parades, birthdays, and holidays

DESCRIPTION
With a unique ability to always look on the grim side, Blake thrives on bumming people out. A question as harmless as whether he likes seafood may provoke him to share that he was eating crab cakes when his parents told him they were separating. (This happened when he was 27.) And he actually prefers movies where the dog does die in the end. (He says it's more true to life.) Blake doesn't believe in silver linings, but he did like to send you articles about how the silver fillings in your mouth contain levels of mercury that are iffy at best. He could be thoughtful sometimes, though. When you got a big promotion at work, he gave you flowers—along with a sympathy card for the loss of what little free time you had.

NESTING
Blake has only ever invited a partner to live with him once. He described it as "cohabitating temporarily until we are ready to break up".

FIG 43: *Blake*

FIG 44: *Zach*

Zach

aka The Older Guy Who Still Acts Like A Younger Guy

NOTABLE BEHAVIORS
Taking his time growing up

DESCRIPTION
Zach's advanced age may seem like a draw. He is known as a "silver fox" and possesses a designated trimmer for his nose and ear hair—all signs that suggest a fully matured specimen. But this ex-boyfriend is actually a close relative of The Man Child. He does not need to live with eight random Craigslist roommates ... he just prefers it. And on more than one occasion, you observed him throwing his socks out after wearing them to avoid doing laundry. To be fair, he did have some paternal instincts. He was briefly the dad to a small python before he lost it somewhere in his duplex. That was around the same time you "lost" his number.

APPEARANCE
Zach looks as though he's in pain, but that's only because he recently threw his back out hopping a fence. (He was trying to sneak into a Harry Styles show.)

Xavier

aka The Ex Who Was Too Perfect, Actually

NOTABLE BEHAVIORS
*Pulling his weight; being in touch with his feelings;
practicing impeccable hygiene*

DESCRIPTION
When it comes to boyfriends, Xavier appears to
be the perfect specimen. He is patient and humble.
He actually listens when others speak, instead of
just waiting for the right moment to cut in with a
non sequitur about the Marvel multiverse. He is not
married. And he hardly has any detectable baggage
because he's already worked through it all with a
therapist. In fact, when you were dating Xavier, he
seemed so perfect that there was only one thing to
do—you had to put an immediate end to things.
Obviously, this man was hiding something. You stand
by this conclusion, and there's no possibility that you
should be unpacking it with *your* therapist right now.

MATING RITUALS
As far as researchers know, Xavier is still looking for
someone special to share his life with. Best wishes to
whoever ends up with this creep!

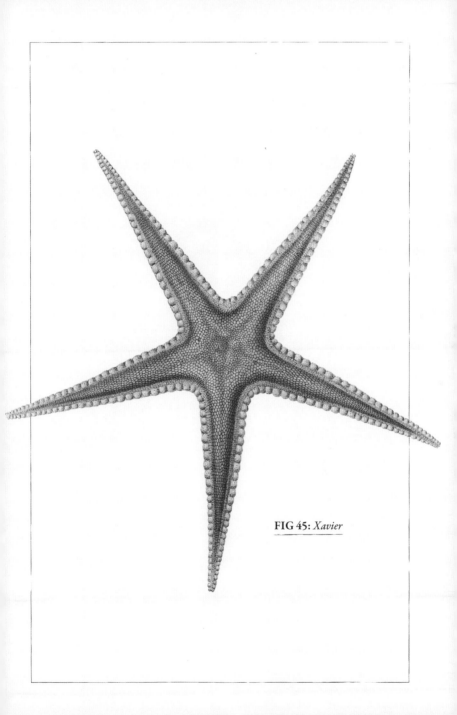

FIG 45: *Xavier*

ABOUT THE AUTHOR

Danielle Kraese is a writer, editor, and retired improviser. She is the co-author of *Jokes to Offend Men*, a modern, feminist take on the classic joke book. Her work has been featured by *The New Yorker*, *McSweeney's Internet Tendency*, *Bustle*, and *Elite Daily*, among other publications. She currently lives and kills plants in the suburbs of Long Island, New York.

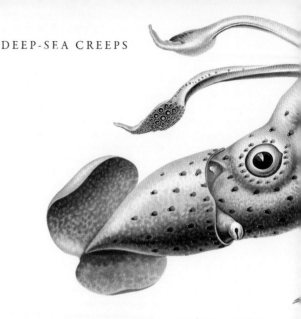

ABOUT THE ILLUSTRATIONS

The majority of the illustrations in this book were created by artists hired by Albert I, Prince of Monaco (1848–1922) to document the findings on his numerous scientific expeditions. Albert I was a dedicated oceanographer who founded the Oceanographic Museum of Monaco and the Oceanographic Institute in Paris. (Not a lot is known about the artists, or their exes).

Published in 2024 by Smith Street Books
Naarm (Melbourne) | Australia
smithstreetbooks.com

ISBN: 978-1-9230-4902-4

Smith Street Books respectfully acknowledges the Wurundjeri People of the
Kulin Nation, who are the Traditional Owners of the land on which we work,
and we pay our respects to their Elders past and present.

Publisher: Hannah Koelmeyer
Editor: Toby Fehily
Design: Andy Warren & Hannah Koelmeyer
Layout: Megan Ellis
Proofreader: Pam Dunne

Printed & bound in China by C&C Offset Printing Co., Ltd.

Book 305
10 9 8 7 6 5 4 3 2 1